MW00896391

Believe 3

For Sam

A poetry collection by John F Connor

Fantastic Books Publishing Edition

ISBN: 978-1523836437

Internal Illustrations by Jolanta Dziok

About John

John Connor was born in 1964 and has been writing poetry since he was sixteen. Following the death of his mother and father, John noticed that his poetry had changed. He wrote to give himself comfort and when he shared his words with others found his poems also gave comfort to them.

Now, with thousands of followers on Facebook and a regular spot writing poetry for a grief management site called 'Healing Hugs', John is surprised at his sudden rise to fame. His work has also appeared on the

'Words of Wisdom' site which currently has over a million followers!

A down to earth family man who dreams of going to America because of his love of 1950s music, John wants his poetry to touch the hearts and souls of those lost in grief.

This is his third collection and he continues to hope that his poetry will inspire and comfort you in your daily life.

10% of the proceeds of this collection will be donated to the grief management site 'Healing Hugs' who do wonderful work helping people all over the world deal with feelings of pain and loss.

Dedication

Most of all I dedicate this collection to my brave wife Sam, who lost her battle with cancer late in 2015.

Along with each and every one of you reading this right now, I dedicate this to the people in my life that have shaped me into the man I am today.

To my mother and father, my brother Colin Connor, sister Debbie Connor and my beautiful sons. You are my world.

I hope you enjoy this collection of poems and that they help you to cope.

John F Connor
December 2015

'I have lived with grief all my life. That's why my poems come straight from the heart. The words just enter my head.'

- John Connor

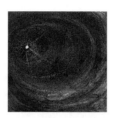

Wish I was a bird on the wing

And sit upon my branch and sing

When I am having a bad day

Just flap my wings and fly away

If you have a cross to bear
Sometimes it helps to share
Even though you are a fighter
Sharing makes the load much
lighter

How I wish all wars would cease

That mankind could live in peace

Lay down your guns and walk

away

I dream about world peace today

How come we can't get along?

How come this planet went so

wrong?

What's the cause of all these wars?

They say their God is better than

yours

Why do we live in a world of hate?

Pretty soon it will be too late

Look at the children, what have we

done?

Why use words when you have a
gun?
Deep inside I feel so sad
This is not the world we could
have had
To love and share, to share and
give
To care about this world we live

I hold your picture in my hand

I try but I can't understand

I see you as you used to be

I wish that you were here with me

I watch you every day

I often see you cry

As you hold on to my picture

And keep asking yourself why

I want to hold you tight

And tell you it's ok

I want to let you know

We will meet again some day

But you cannot hear my words

You cannot feel my touch

But I need you to know

I love you very much

I am there when you awake

I try to keep you strong

I turn the radio up

When they play our song

I hold you in my arms

But I know deep inside you know

That I would find a way

I would not let you go

I want you to be happy

Live the life you have

It hurts to see you cry

It hurts to see you sad

I will never leave you

We will never be apart

If you ever need me

I am right there in your heart

When you smile for no reason

That's the time I know

That you realize

That I would never let you go

And when you go to sleep

I sit beside your bed

I gently stroke your hair
And kiss you on your head
Have sweet dreams my darling
No more dreams of sorrow
I will always be here
Today and tomorrow

If we search into our hearts
We know it will be true
Knowing we will meet again
Helps to see us through
Though we sometimes don't get
chance
To say that last goodbye
Left with emptiness
And a longing to know why
No one can answer questions
Or give reasons why it's so
But loved ones still walk beside us
They never really go
Just believe in heaven
And hold it in your heart
Memories will keep us going
While we are apart

The light will come one day
One day for me and you
Those we have loved and lost
Will be there to guide us through
Live, love and be happy
Each sunrise and sunset
Don't dwell on grief and sorrow
Heart ache and regret

Death is just a sunset

So do not dwell on sorrow

Darkness will soon pass

The sun will rise again tomorrow

You need to get over it

You've been grieving for too long

Time to put it behind you

Time that you moved on

How I hate these words

They don't know how I feel

I am not seeking attention

The pain inside is real

I did not choose to feel this way

But my heart was broken in two

I was left in a world of pain

I did not know what to do

Too scared to say your name

For fear of what they'd say

I am trying my best

But the pain will always stay
Everyone will grieve
It's just a part of life
Everyone will grieve
Be it child, husband or wife
We all will do it our way
That's the way it has to be
No one else can stop this
It's all down to me
I will deal with it
Alone, in my own time
There will be good and bad days
Surely that's not a crime
It won't happen overnight
Yes, it may take years
Yes, I may lock myself away
And cry a lot of tears
But one day I will get there

And learn to move along

It's my right to grieve

It's natural, not wrong

How I wish I had a magic wand

To take away your pain

To banish all your sadness

And make you smile once again

If you knock me down I will get
back up
I will not stay down for long
I will learn from mistakes I make
in life
I will use them to make me strong
Sometimes it's just so easy
To give in and walk away
But I will stand my ground
It's just a game we all must play
When you reach the bottom
And feel you have run out of luck
For when you reach the bottom
The only way is up
Time to dust yourself down

Time to start anew
This is your life and yours alone
This one belongs to you

Tomorrow is another chance

Yesterdays they go so fast

Start living for the future

Stop living in the past

Everyone has a dream

A place they want to be

Don't let others tell you what to do

Be strong, be proud, be free

Every sunset ends a day

Every sunrise, a new day begun

Days, weeks, months and years

move fast

So cherish every one

Time goes by in the blink of an eye

Life's clock forever tick tocks

Don't dwell on what you don't
have
Be grateful with what you've got
When you are in life's storms
And cannot see a way through
Remember behind the darkest
clouds
There awaits a sky so blue

Do you sit on a fluffy cloud
As happy as can be?
Do you spend all your time
Watching over me?
Do you help me through the day?
Do you help to keep me strong?
Do you leave me little signs
To show you have not gone?
When I say your name
Do you know it's you I seek?
Do you ever leave your cloud
To put butterfly kisses on my
cheek?

If you spend your life looking back

How can you move on?

Those days are in the past

They're history, they're gone

Now the future matters

For the future is all we have

Better to wear a smile

Than sit there feeling sad

Memories will never fade

They live in our hearts forever

Enjoy the life you have

One day we will be together

I draw my heart on glass

In the hope that you can see

Sending you all my love

To heaven just from me

If you take from life

But never give

You will never know

What it's like to live

It takes one moment

To show you care

It takes one moment

To give, to share

When you see pain

Do not walk away

A 'how are you?'

Could make their day

No one knows

How life can be

That man on the street

Could be you or me
Count your blessings
For what you have
And you will realize
Life is not so bad

I hate it when you cry
But you don't understand
I am sitting right beside you
I am there, I hold your hand
I would never leave you
Surely inside you know
That I will wait forever
Because I love you so
I am there when you awake
I am there when you sleep at night
Though you do not feel it
I often hold you tight
Sometimes you look so lost
Staring into space
Wondering where I am

Am I in a happy place?

Yes, I am happy

I want you to know that's true

Do you know why I am happy?

Because I spend my days with you

I know you do not see me
Or hear the words I say
But you don't realize
I am never far away
I guide you through your days
With words your soul does hear
I hug you when you cry
I wipe away the tear
When you sleep at night
I sit upon your bed
I say sleep tight my darling
And kiss you on your head
When you feel a chill
Or a shadow you can see
I leave you little signs

To know that it is me
So no more tears my angel
Just live the life god gave
I will be right beside you
Be strong, be proud, be brave

No one knows how long we have

The future is unclear

Be grateful for each day

Be grateful you are here

Live life for the moment

Live life for the day

To ponder on the future

Is to throw your life away

From the moment you wake up

To start a brand new day

Treat it like your last

It's best to live that way

Don't ponder on the what ifs

Don't ponder on what might have

been

While you are here still living
You can still fulfill that dream

Learn what is important
Not money, cars and wealth
The things that really matter
Are family, friends and health
Tomorrow is never guaranteed
So live, love and be strong
Learn from your mistakes
Walk tall and carry on
Life is just a test
To learn, to share and love
Everything we learn in life
We take with us up above

It's my grief, it's my fight
Only I will know when the time is
right
I know you are trying to help with
the words you say
But I have to do this my own way
No two people grieve the same
We shout, we scream, we cry, we
blame
Sometimes people don't
understand
Speak words of comfort and hold
my hand
But deep inside the pain is real
The outside world doesn't know
how I feel
The big dark cloud won't go away
Blocking out my sunny day
But I will never give up this fight
Until I know the time is right
Just stay with me and show you
care

It helps sometimes to know you're
there
Don't be scared to say their name
For fear that you might cause me
pain
I like to remember how things
used to be
So share your memories with me
Time will pass and I may heal
But I cannot help the way I feel
Yes, sometimes I may stare into
space
Find myself lost in another place
Grief will come to all in time
But right now this grief is mine

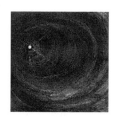

I will never give up
I will never give in
I will weather this storm
In the end, I will win
For I will not quit
When things go wrong
I will pick myself up
I will learn and carry on
I will not moan
I will not shout
I will sit and think
Till I work it out
I will not feel sorry
Or down on my luck
I am stronger than this
I will never give up

When you are at your lowest
And running out of luck
Remember from the bottom
The only way is up

With every breath of air you
breathe
Make the most of what you have
Better to wear a smile on your face
Than it is to frown and be sad

No one has all the answers
To the questions on your mind
You may search a lifetime
But the answers you won't find
So don't look for the answers
Just live life for the day
To spend a lifetime thinking
Is a lifetime passed away

A true friend has a listening ear
A true friend has a caring heart
A true friend will always think of
you
Whenever you are apart
A true friend always understands
The things that you go through
A true friend never questions
things
They're always there for you
A true friend speaks from the
heart
And will listen to what you say
A true friend will always be there
When others walk away

A true friend is rare

I know that to be true

But I know I am blessed

To have a true friend like you

My guardian angel walks beside
me
Never far away
My guardian angel guides me
Each and every day
I know I am never alone
For my angel is always near
I know my angel loves me
I have nothing to fear
For I believe in angels
For I know it's true
Everyone has an angel
They help us to get through
Though we may never see them
Or hear the words they say

They are sent to guide us
Each and every day
Your angel could be a loved one
Someone you miss dear
Who became your guardian angel
They stayed with you right here
Ask them for their help
And you will be heard
For your guardian angel
Hears your every word
When you are feeling down
And don't know what to do
Remember your guardian angel
Is always there for you

I feel I am sitting behind a wall

I am just sitting there on a chair

I feel that I am alone

And no one else is there

This wall is my grief

Yes, this wall is mine

Only I can take it down

But only one brick at a time

I hear people on the other side

Trying to get in

But this is a battle

That only I can win

I need to be alone a while

To think my feelings through

To learn to live with my grief

To work out what to do
I hear the words they say
I know they love me so
But this is a healing process
I have to take it slow
Time will pass, I will learn
I will grow strong
And when the time is right
My wall will be gone
Until then bear with me
Be with me all the way
One day this storm will lift
To reveal a sunny day

I woke up this morning
And thought that it is time
That I enjoyed again
This life of mine
No more self pity
Sadness and sorrow
Going to live each day
Like there's no tomorrow
I am all done with crying
My tears have all gone
Need to get my act together
I need to grow strong
I will shout from the hill tops
I'm so glad I'm alive
I am stronger than life
And I will survive

Do you sit upon a cloud
As happy as can be?
Do you spend your days
Watching over me?

There is a dark cloud above my
head
That will not go away
Following me everywhere
Blocking my sunny day
But it won't last forever
I know that to be true
Over time that cloud gets smaller
And reveals a sky of blue

A mother's love is strong

A mother's love is pure

A mother's love is deep

A mother's love is so much more

A mother's love is giving

A mother's love is fair

A mother's love is worry

A mother's love is care

A mother's love is to be there

A mother's love is words so true

A mother's love will always guide

you

A mother's love will get you

through

A mother's love will give you

strength

A mother's love will last forever

A mother's love has no distance

A mother's love keeps you together

A mother's love will never fade

A mother's love will make you

strong

A mother's love will last forever

Even when your mother's gone

Cancer is a different grief
Cancer's so unfair
With cancer you are grieving
For someone who's still there
You have to fight for two
But where do you begin?
You cannot give up the fight
Though the battle is hard to win
Sometimes it gets so hard
As you watch them feel the pain
Hoping and praying every day
It does not return again
You have to search for inner
strength
Wherever that may be
For I know what it feels like
For it happened to me

These words flow so easy
Straight from my broken heart
Something happened in my life
That tore my world apart
I never saw it coming
Came right out of the blue
Left me sitting shell shocked
Not knowing what to do
Never known pain like it
Don't know where to start
How will I ever get over
And mend this broken heart?
At first I spoke to no one
Just sat there all alone
Not wanting to go out
Never leaving my home
People offered comfort

Flowers, maybe a card
But this pain was new to me
I found it really hard
Just sat there looking at pictures
Of how it used to be
Going over the memories
Of when you were here with me
Days they turned to weeks
Weeks they turned to years
I had done so much soul searching
Cried so many tears
One day I found the strength
To walk outside the door
I know deep in my heart
You would want me to live once
more
I knew it would not be easy
But something I had to do
I knew that you would guide me
And help to get me through

Grief it has no time scale
Each one has their own
You cannot help or rush them
They have to do it on their own
Over time the pain will heal
Over time I will grow strong
I know I must never give in
I need to carry on
I know I have but one life
And things don't always go to plan
But learning from my past
Makes me the person that I am

Follow that dream
And never let go
It just might come true
You just never know
We all need a dream
It's what keeps us going
Part of the battle
Is not ever knowing
Sometimes a dream
Is a golden sand beach
But try as you may
It seems out of your reach
But never give in
And never surrender
Dreams can come true
You just need to remember
Dreams give us hope

Dreams make us wish
For the things that we want
And the people we miss
Everyone has a dream
A wish to come true
The dream's in your reach
It's all up to you

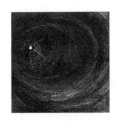

Every so often I look up to the sky

Looking for answers and

wondering why

The meaning of life, why am I

here?

Sometimes for knowledge,

sometimes out of fear

We are so small in the universe's

eye

So many thoughts as I look up to

the sky

There must be a planet wherever it

may be

With someone watching the sky

and thinking like me

I am trying my best
To remain strong
But it's not that easy
Now that you've gone
I'm lost and alone
What can I do?
I am finding it hard
To go on without you
You were my soul mate
My best friend, my lover
You were my life
Just you and no other
I miss your smile
How things used to be
I was so happy
When you were with me

It saddens me to see you blue

It saddens me to see you cry

I know it will be hard

But my darling you must try

I know you think you have lost me

But my darling that's not true

Though you do not see me

I am always here with you

I hug you when you cry

I lie beside you at night

Teardrops on your pillow

I am there, I hold you tight

Did you think I would leave?

You know that is not true

You are forever my soul mate

It's a bond I share with you
Just because you cannot see me
Or hear the words I say

If you search inside your heart

You will know I'm never far away

I know you have to grieve

But please don't grieve too long

Soon you will realise

I am here, I have not gone

There is so much more to life

For now I know it's true

That's why I spend my time

Watching over you

One day you will understand

Till then live the life you have

I want to see you happy

It hurts to see you sad

There are no words that I can say

To help to take the pain away

But there is one thing I can do

I will always be there for you

A shoulder to cry on, a listening

ear

When you need me I will be here

I lost my smile I don't know where

Checked the mirror, it's not there

I lost my smile, I don't know why

All I seem to do is cry

I lost my smile, inside I'm sad

I remember the smile I used to

have

But when I learn to deal with this

pain

I will get it back again

Fly my little angel fly

Way up to the sky

Fly up past the clouds

To heaven way up high

Be free my little angel

For no one is ever late

When you get to heaven

They will be waiting at the gate

Rest my little angel

For your days on earth are done

You were loved so much

By me and everyone

Rest my little angel

You know that I will grieve

But my heart knows where you are

I know because I believe

Miss you my little angel

As you watch over me

Your earth body has ceased

Your soul released, fly free

Miss you little angel

But it won't be forever

For what heaven takes apart

Heaven puts back together

Love you little angel

More than you will know

It's hard to say goodbye

It's hard to let you go

Peace my little angel

Now and forever

When the time is right

I know we will be together

Don't say goodbye

For that is wrong

Don't say goodbye

I have not gone

Don't say goodbye

For I am still here

Don't say goodbye

I am always near

Don't say goodbye

I am here with you

Don't say goodbye

I will help you through

Don't say goodbye

I am never far away

Don't say goodbye

I am there each day
Don't say goodbye
Though you don't see
Don't say goodbye
I am here, it's me
Don't say goodbye
It is not true
Don't say goodbye
I would never leave you
Don't say goodbye
I am somewhere greater
It's not goodbye
But see you later

How do you fight something

That you cannot see?

That hurting someone

Who's so close to me

How do you stay strong

When you cannot win?

You cannot see it on their face

As it hides deep within

Some won't say your name

They call you the big C

But I want you to know

That you do not scare me

You might win this fight

But you won't win this war

We will fight the big fight

You won't take anymore
Mothers and fathers
Daughters and kin
Whatever it takes
It's a war we must win
You entered my life
And caused me such pain
But enough is enough
You won't do it again
You think I am weak
You will find I am strong
You think you can break me
I will prove that you're wrong
Let us unite
For the battle's begun
And we will not give up
Until this war is won
So hide in the shadows

Like a coward you hide

You have no shame

You have no pride

But hear my words

For my heart is true

This evil called cancer

I am coming for you

Believe in heaven

With all your heart

And you will never

Be apart

Believe in angels

And you will find

Love and hope

And peace of mind

Fly free my angel
Fly free, fly high
It's see you later
It's not goodbye

My love for you will never die

My love will never cease

Though it hurts inside

I know you are at peace

I know we share a bond

That ties our souls together

A bond formed out of love

A bond that lasts forever

I know you are never far

I know that you are near

Though I cannot see you

My heart knows you are here

I will learn from my mistakes
Know where I went wrong
Remember what doesn't kill you
Can only make you strong

Sometimes I find myself

Just staring into space

No sounds and no movement

Just in another place

Deep in thought and wonder

Where time stands still a while

Replaying memories in my mind

My face becomes a smile

My memories are my escape

They stay with me forever

I know that at any time

I can replay a time together

I can choose a special moment

Or a very special day

Like a CD in my head

In my mind I just press play

You are never far away

I know you are with me

I know you sit and watch

When I replay a memory

You are the waves that crash upon

the shore

You are the wind that blows

through the trees

You are the golden sunset

You are the summer breeze

You are a child's laughter

You are the birds that sing

You are autumn and winter

You are summer and you are

spring

You are the golden sun

You are the moon and night

You are the green fields I roam

You are the stars that shine so

bright

You are the air I breathe

You are my heart that beats inside

You are every emotion I feel

You are love and hope and pride

You are everything

You are near yet oh so far

But everywhere I look

I know is where you are

Crying is good

Crying is not wrong

Crying just means

You have been strong for far too

long

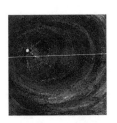

Walking in darkness

No light can be seen

Not really knowing

If it's real or just a dream

Each day is a blur

Each day is the same

Tears in my eyes

And a heart full of pain

They all try to help

They say I'll be ok

That the pain will ease

With each passing day

Grief is so real

It is there in my head

From the moment I wake

Till I go to my bed
Even in sleep
It is there in my dreams
I just want to shout
I just want to scream
But I need to be brave
I need to be strong
And fight this battle
No matter how long
I must fight for myself
And do what is right
Till the darkness lifts
To reveal the light
I will grow stronger
I will grow, I will learn
We all will fight grief
And now it's my turn

I watch you every day
I am always very near
I know deep in your heart
You realize I am here
I watch you while you asleep
In your bed at home
I hear you when you speak to me
When you are on your own
You cannot understand
The reason why I have gone
But I will never leave you
I am there to keep you strong
Talk to me, I hear you
Though you may not see
We share an unbroken bond
That will always be
Death won't keep us apart

For our love is forever
Just remember me in your heart
And one day we'll be together
Live your life and live it full
Don't waste a single day
Remember I'm always with you
I will never go away

I am a child's laughter
I am the red, red rose
I am the butterfly kisses
You feel upon your nose
I am the golden sunset
I am the stars at night
Believe what's in your heart
And you will be alright

Publisher's note

When I first met John it was via a telephone meeting about publishing his first collection of poetry 'Believe'. It was clear from that point that this man had something magical about him. We spoke about his inspiration and how he creates his poems and he explained that in most cases he is simply relaxing at home or out in the garden and an unquenchable urge to write overtakes him. He talked about the feeling that these poems would suddenly announce themselves in his head and he simply had to write them down.

He told me that he wanted to get his words out to as many people suffering from grief and heartache as he could.

Next came John's second collection 'Believe 2' in which John's poetry was joined by the inspirational illustrations of Jolanta Dziok.

This latest collection holds a special place in my heart because John's wife Sam, who had been battling with cancer during the final phases of putting this, John's largest ever collection, together, sadly lost her battle before it could be released.

It is my sincere hope that John's own poetry and the support of his fans from around the world will help him come to terms with his own grief in the same way as he has helped countless others in similar situations to his own.

John's healing poetry has already been an inspiration for millions of people, from all backgrounds, from all over the world. His simple, heartfelt style reflects his own personality as a helpful, friendly and wonderful person.
It has been a privilege to publish John's work and to help him get his inspirational poetry out to the world.

I sincerely hope you have enjoyed this, his third collection, and will recommend it to your friends.

Thank you.

Dan Grubb
CEO
Fantastic Books Publishing

Made in the USA
Columbia, SC
30 May 2019